youthwriterscamp.com

Greetings to All!

Welcome to those who have decided to give this young author's first book a read. We believe in youth and their stories so much that we believe we can be a part of helping them tell their stories. We have been so inspired to see them grow and change.

Our Youth Writers Camp provides continuous opportunities for healthy emotional expression within a safe and supportive community. Our goal is to both to help young people cope through writing and to motivate them to develop their own streams of revenue.

Brandon C Allen, LLC is actively engaging today's youth with an aim to increase mental and emotional health outcomes. However, we understand that our efforts to positively impact the mental and emotional health of this current generation won't reach maximum effectiveness unless we have the support of the entire community.

THIS IS WHERE YOU COME IN.

Through the things they discovered about themselves, the lessons about mental health, and the coping techniques they garnered during this time, it is our job as a community to continue to cultivate their development and empower them to shift their own realities into the best versions designed for them. Our hope is that these students feel loved, cared for, and equipped enough to continue to heal and process with healthy coping tools and creative avenues. Thank you for investing in this student, one poem at a time.

Students, congratulations and I am proud of all you accomplished. Continue to be all you are meant to be.

Brandon Allen, Author and Founder of Youth Writers Camp

Dear Shaniese,

Do you know what you just did? Seriously. Think about it. You wrote your first book. Did you know that a recent survey of 2,000 U.S. respondents reveals just 15 percent have started writing a book, and a mere six percent have gotten halfway through?

You beat the odds. Many say what they are going to do. Some start it, then abandon it—very few finish. You finished.

Growing up, I always kept a journal. Writing and playing the piano were my first loves. Had I known of a program like this and had a teacher like Brandon Allen, I would have been an author at seven years old. Serving alongside Brandon and making many young authors' dreams come true is a blessing.

Remember, this is just your first step in a long and adventurous journey. Always write. Writing can serve as a constant and reliable best friend.

With love and poetry,

Camari Carter Hawkins

Author and Founder of Mama's Kitchen Press

The Rooms I Live In

Shaniese Armstrong

MAMA'S
KITCHEN
PRESS

The Rooms I Live In
©2023 Shaniese Armstrong
ISBN: 979-8-9893829-2-7

First Edition, 2023

Printed in the United States of America

Cover Concept by Shaniese Armstrong
Cover & Layout Design by Emily Anne Evans

Contents

Foreword

Not being heard is no reason for silence.
~Les Misérables

It is the way my daughter's eyes gleamed with excitement and wonder when she listened intently to every word spoken while a story was being told. How she gazed and took in every single detail of a movie or show she watched. Not to mention the hundreds of books, scripts, plays, novels, short stories...and any other form of literature that she has constantly devoured. Mostly, it is the way Shaniese tells a story that made it certain writing was in her future.

The Rooms I Live In is the first of many books to come. I am both proud and honored to be writing this foreword. We are nothing but fortunate to be able to experience Shaniese's creative mind, witnessing her work as it blossoms and evolves throughout her life's journey is but a gift for us all.

Taking any step forward is a job well done. I am eager to watch her grow as a writer, as a woman, and as an incredible human. It takes great courage to put yourself out there and allow others to experience your creativeness. Shaniese is a woman who stands securely in her uniqueness. I have no doubt that her poetry will exhibit much of her quirky delightfulness.

Thank you for not being silent, Shaniese.

La Kiesha Armstrong

The
Rooms
I Live In

Entry

Picture-perfect pictures on the wall
Pristine cushions on prestige couches
A bell jar full of fake candy inside a crystal glass
Waiting to be perceived
Welcome to the house
Haunted by my childhood ghost
Inhumane lurkers of the shadow
Warnings before immersing yourselves
In the decrepit part of town
Don't stare too long at the shadows
They get shy and may lash out
Don't idle about
Things and people vanish
I have yet to find what was lost
Don't whisper in front of a mirror
They might whisper back
And finally, always lock your door
Although it does very little to keep them out

Dining Room

Dinner is served at the stroke of midnight
Untouched grand dinner adorns the dining table
Head chair pristine, gaudy, untouched
The other chairs scrape the floor
Worn from the starving occupants
Waiting to be served
For permission to consume
The head waits five minutes till the 13th hour
Creaky joints limp down the aisle to sit
Finally, the 13th hour
The ravenous monsters hark above the feast
Be quick, it will disappear within the hour
You hear someone or something whisper
Every night it is like this
Every night you do not eat

Kitchen

Be hypervigilant, you may never know what is a weapon
Or poisonous
This may seem like an ordinary place of food preparation
Although the cabinetry is locked up
The fridge is free to use
Don't be alarmed by the ghosts
Ghouls
And the undead that reside in here
They tend to leave guests alone

Closet Mirror

When I look into the mirror, it isn't me I see
The person looking back is a shapeshifter
Blending into the crowd, trying so hard not to stand out
The person in the mirror looks distorted
Eyes too dark
Lips in a downwards tic
Teeth too sharp
Most days I can barely stand to look before I am dressed
So in the closet I go to create something to be perceived
The closet is too deep
Scared of what's coming in
Petrified of what will come out
Most days I can hear the whispers
{Come in we will protect you}
What an odd way to comfort me from the mirror

Living Room

Around the clock

TV does not take a break from filling the silence

Stuck in a rotation of ignorance and rambunctious energy

It can be heard from anywhere in the house

Brainwashing you to believe nothing is worse

Than going outside

If you listen closely, you can hear the whispers of victims

Trapped in a faux reality

Listen too much

Your mind will be lulled to never leave

A certain comfort in the mindlessness of this room

Boogie Man

When you decided that I was not worthy of feeling
I agreed
When you shoved me into my room and locked the door
I pretended to be someone who needed saving
I believed nothing was scarier than the Boogie Man
At least he allowed me to feel whole-heartedly
At least he protected me from the harshness of your world
You taught me to survive
He taught me to love me
You taught me to hide
He taught me how to use my greatest strengths
You taught me pain
He taught me peace
He protected me through the night
Listened to me cry
Showed me kindness that I didn't think existed
How is it that the actual monster was you?

Library

In this decrepit place you can find
Knowledge of the worlds
But be careful of what lurks between the bookshelves
They may watch from a safe distance
They are always foreboding
When you see one, keep your eyes down
Appear to be smaller
Don't run or make a sound
Hopefully they will pass you by
If you don't
If you look them in their nightmarish eye
The sinister smile will trap you

Balcony

I did it
I jumped
I was blinded by the sun
It melted my trauma like wax into my skin
All I was trying to do was fall in love with me
Next thing I know my angel and
My demon rock me to sleep
Whispering sweet nothings in my ear
Every night
Holding me tightly till morning
And through the evening
I don't believe in the warnings they give me
I know there is a whole world waiting to get to know me
All I was trying to do was fall in love with me
So I did it, I jumped
Free-falling
Falling for so long, I'm starting to enjoy the view
It's a lot prettier than looking for the next impact
Falling for so long, the wax is starting to crack
I didn't realize I was already flying
Falling for so long, I no longer have the fear of landing

Distance

The distance between you and me is separated by a wall
And yet you cannot reach
But then again, you didn't even try
Stuck listening to your belligerent yells
My room became a barricade
Hypervigilant in protecting myself
I didn't let anyone in
I didn't go out of my barricades
Waiting for you to blow up
Why must I become a bigger person?

Portal

My portal is voice-activated
Speak soliloquies
It will be forever flowing like Niagara Falls
Be careful not to drown in my depths
As the cadence of your voice powers it up
To make your journey that much enjoyable
My portal's ecosystem is sensitive
It doesn't accept trivial human things
Barely accepting some waters
Not nourishing it can disrupt
The whole system out of whack
My portal has only two destinations:
My garden, which has my mind
Heart
And soul
The weather is always nice
With a few rainy days to snuggle up
Or my purgatory where my monsters
My most sadistic sides reside

About the Author

I was born in Fontana, California January 20th, 2000.
As a young girl I forced myself to be brave and not need
a nightlight to sleep. Now that I am older I wish for the
same bravery as my younger self — the first step is
publishing this book. I have been writing since I was 16,
mostly writing novels. This is my first poetry book.

www.ingramcontent.com/pod-product-compliance
Lightning Source LLC
Chambersburg PA
CBHW060509300726
48975CB00008B/2719